Tricky Chaos

Megan Clough

BookLeaf Publishing

India | USA | UK

Presentation by *BookLeaf Publishing*

Web: www.bookleafpub.com

E-mail: info@bookleafpub.com

ISBN: 9789360945435

First edition 2024

My love letter to all the wonderful weirdos.

PREFACE

When the ups and downs of our daily struggles take hold, there will be something in here for a moment of joy. Take something from this book to help you feel as though whatever the weather, someone relates, and brighter days are ahead.

A Bowl of Optimism

I have a bowl full of hope and promise, and it's overflowing with abundance.

I carry it with me all day but sometimes set it aside.

I can carry it for longer but it gets a little heavy and sometimes I forget the bowl is somewhere around.

And when it's been too long,
I search frantically again
This time the contents are hard to hold because the bowl became a seive.

So I cry at the loss and render my contents gone.

Then I shake myself up and get to sweeping the up again.

I put them in my bowl and some of its gone forever, but here I find some new things swept up along the way.

Cured!

If you find yourself sad beyond belief
Try this remedy for some temporary relief

Wiggle your toes, yep still there
Bend your knees, if they hurt just swear
And move your hips one side to the other
And pull your shoulders up to the air
And scrunch your fingers in your hair

Well done for doing it, though the instructions were brief
No doubt you look silly and are laughing in disbelief.

Absent

3

True to form here I am absent again
My mind is an exhausting job to maintain
So hopefully you will see the days I give more
than I am meant
In exchange for a few lacklustre days in bed

Burnt out

I excelled a job and they gave me a promotion
Then work was too chaotic and caused intense
emotion
After giving all I could to do the locomotion
I was exhausted and drained amongst all the
commotion
I'm suddenly struck by a wild notion
If this job is so bad, why am I scared of
demotion?
So I told them to shove it, they don't deserve my
devotion.

Polished

5

I wish I was someone with polished perfect nails
And shiny hair that is meant for enviable
ponytails
I wish I took more pride in having pristine
eyebrows
And wore ironed clothes from posh branded
labels
I wish I made time to put more effort in
But here I am amongst my collected trash
wondering where to put my paint tin

Later

6

Mirror mirror, leaned up against the wall
I forgot to put you up and you've been there
since fall
I'll get round to you some day soon
But right now I must lay in the bath and prune

Hold the ladder

I love to see people succeed
I watch their wins like shooting stars
Fleeting, but magically freed
A moment I have witnessed from the start
It's not that often people chase dreams
So when they do I take it to heart
I ponder on it then roll up my sleeves
And dream about my name next to their business
cards

NOT my card

8

Magicians are my nemesis
I expect you will want me to preface this
They are simply lyers with a God complex
On the street, in a show... Menaces

The rest

Time to rest
But first I will put the washing on
Time to rest
But then I just need to clean up the kitchen
Time to rest
But I better just hoover the mess from earlier
Time to rest
But I best just sort out that warning letter first
Time to rest
But I didn't take the bins out!
Time to rest
But I haven't even showered!
Time to rest
I needed to go to the shop, I'll go now
Time to rest
I need to clean this stuff out of the fridge
Time to rest
I need a drink I'm parched.. And hungry!
Time to rest
I was supposed to take a parcel
Time to rest
If I don't sort my lunch out now I won't in the
morning
Time to... Go to bed it's very late!

I will have to do the rest tomorrow.

Cosy

It's warm and cosy in here
Down in the front room with you dear
But down your eyelids do creep
I can see you falling asleep
Go to bed, I say in a gentle tone
My words are greeted with a snappy groan
GET TO BED! You can't sleep there, I exclaim
But I'm warm and cosy here, you say.
It just won't be the same!

Glow

I'm looking for my glow
I swear I had it yesterday
The dark has crept in quietly
Before I had chance to know
My glow lit up the room
I was so illuminating
Now I need a torch or lighter
To navigate this blackout
Not a spark to stop me from ruminating
Now just a candle flickers toward the abyss
So I close my eyes and try to remember
It's not always... Like this.

Moat

I built an enormous moat around my mind
To contain my castle of thoughts within
I would only drop the drawbridge if you swear
to be kind
Stoney, tall and warm from the sun
The foundations are crude, I didn't know how to
start
They are rough, mismatched and uneven
The next ones were tightly packed, I had gotten
down to a fine art

Then there were some laid with initials in, from
all those helpers along the way
They weren't work shy, but became ever more
curious
They taught me to take a break and pick it up
another day
I used to guard this moat fiercely defending my
strong fortress
But the longer my helpers stayed, I could no
longer say
Why I shouldn't let them in, when not one minds
the mess

Embarrassed? Me?

It truly is a puzzle to me
When people lack the nerve to be free
'I wouldn't dare do that'
But why? What's holding you back?
'I can't do that they will laugh'
So make them laugh?
'I can't let anyone see me like this'
Well you are not as bad as rubbish killing fish?!
'I can't, I couldn't, I wouldn't, how embaressing'

Are you saying that I am all those negatives?
Are you laughing at me? Are you embarrassed
for me?

If the answer is yes, then good, enjoy from a
distance.

But oh,
if the answer is no
then join me,
step into the freedom of living life the way you
dream instead of tiptoeing around the entrance.

Ode to a tired woman

Do you need a hand? I am here to help!
Do need some help? I am here on hand!

Do I need some help? (yes)
"no I'm just fine!"
Do I need a hand? (yes)
"no I'm just grand!"

Chit chat

15

Thank you friend, for asking how I was
So often I forget I am not meant to keep it on
lock
And you? I asked, and you truly were kind
You shared a problem you too had been
tormented by
Well look at us, two peas in a pod!
So easily this could have been just a smile and a
nod
But now we both feel lighter and the day is
nearly gone
But tomorrow we should do this again,
I think this talking thing might catch on

Later, again

I see you there water bottle, with a judgemental
undertone
Yes it's been hours of me scrolling my phone
But if you think for one second I'm moving for a
sip
It would be more likely for you to levitate to my
lip
OK fine perhaps you are right
I am thirsty, I said it, let's not need fight
So I'll pick you up just as soon I next move
From the spot on my chair where my bum has
made a groove

Can't sing

I have a song in my heart but by no means can I
sing.
I try to project it out for all to see.

I incessantly chatter trying to explain it
Craft it with paper to see if I can make it
Years spent preparing to sketch or paint it
I strum the ukulele and attempt to play it
Sometimes I even try to bake it
Choreograph a dance but I can't shake it
There is no other way for me to recreate it.

Perhaps it's time to accept that my song is there
to stay.

Resolutions

Here is my list of resolutions
That I hope are to be solutions
Ahead is my year of evolution
So I will start with task distribution
I vow to strictly perform my ablutions
And keep to them in regular volution
I promise to speak in fine elocution
To stop sharing my wild delusions
(which will keep me out of institutions)
I will see jobs through to fine execution
To finally experience some absolution
I will seek out hope and dream restitution
And avoid crumbling into dissolution
To clear a thought path free of pollution,
I won't seek out other's contribution,
protecting my mind from convolution
Now comes the time to share my worst
attribution.
These rules I have instated have inspired my
revolution.
And although they are wrote down, there's no
risk of prosecution
Yet again I am plagued with my own self
persecution.

How does one complete the year without need
for retribution.

19

Paused

I love my friends dearly
Though I forget to prioritise all of their feelings
I think about the things they have said and
giggle to myself
It feels in that moment like they are right there
with me
I hope they carry me too, and think of me just as
fondly
Because their impression on my heart is there
permanently
So I hope they forgive me when I don't reach out
promptly
I have to take some time alone to rescue my
sanity
I've found lots of hobbies to heal my anxiety
But I am here I promise, and I will be back
shortly.

Avoiding the void

I lie on the bed, hair still damp and wrapped
Trying to push past the feeling that my energy is
zapped
It's been one thing after another of life trying to
get the better
So excuse me if I don't seem to be the usual go
getter
I just need a while to figure out my game plan
So leave me alone until I decide it's time to stand

So long

Toodle oo
Toodle oh
Toodle ew

Whatever you prefer,
'tis goodbye to you

www.ingramcontent.com/pod-product-compliance
Lightning Source LLC
LaVergne TN
LVHW050507210726

843509LV00015BA/3027